COLOR UP THE SPECTRUM

Compiled and Designed by Heather Down

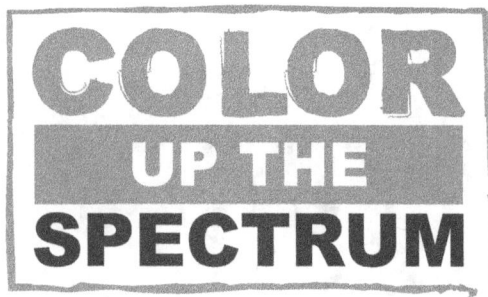

ISBN 978-1-894813-84-6

Published by Echo Books, an imprint of Wintertickle Press
132 Commerce Park Drive, Unit K, Suite 155
Barrie, ON, Canada L4N 0Z7

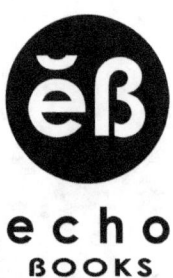

echo
BOOKS

fb/winterticklepress
winterticklepress.com

For Logan, of course.

Introduction

Whether a parent, teacher, caregiver, brother, sister, grandparent or bus driver of someone on the spectrum, you know how incredibly awesome a person diagnosed with Autism is. You are also probably equally aware that sometimes there are challenges. Understanding, acceptance, coping strategies, and education are all helpful.

My grandson is on the spectrum, and he inspires me every day. It is my hope that this little book can provide some quiet time to color and reflect. Go ahead, color up the spectrum!

"AWE-tism"

- Author Unknown

"I am different, not less."

- Temple Grandin,

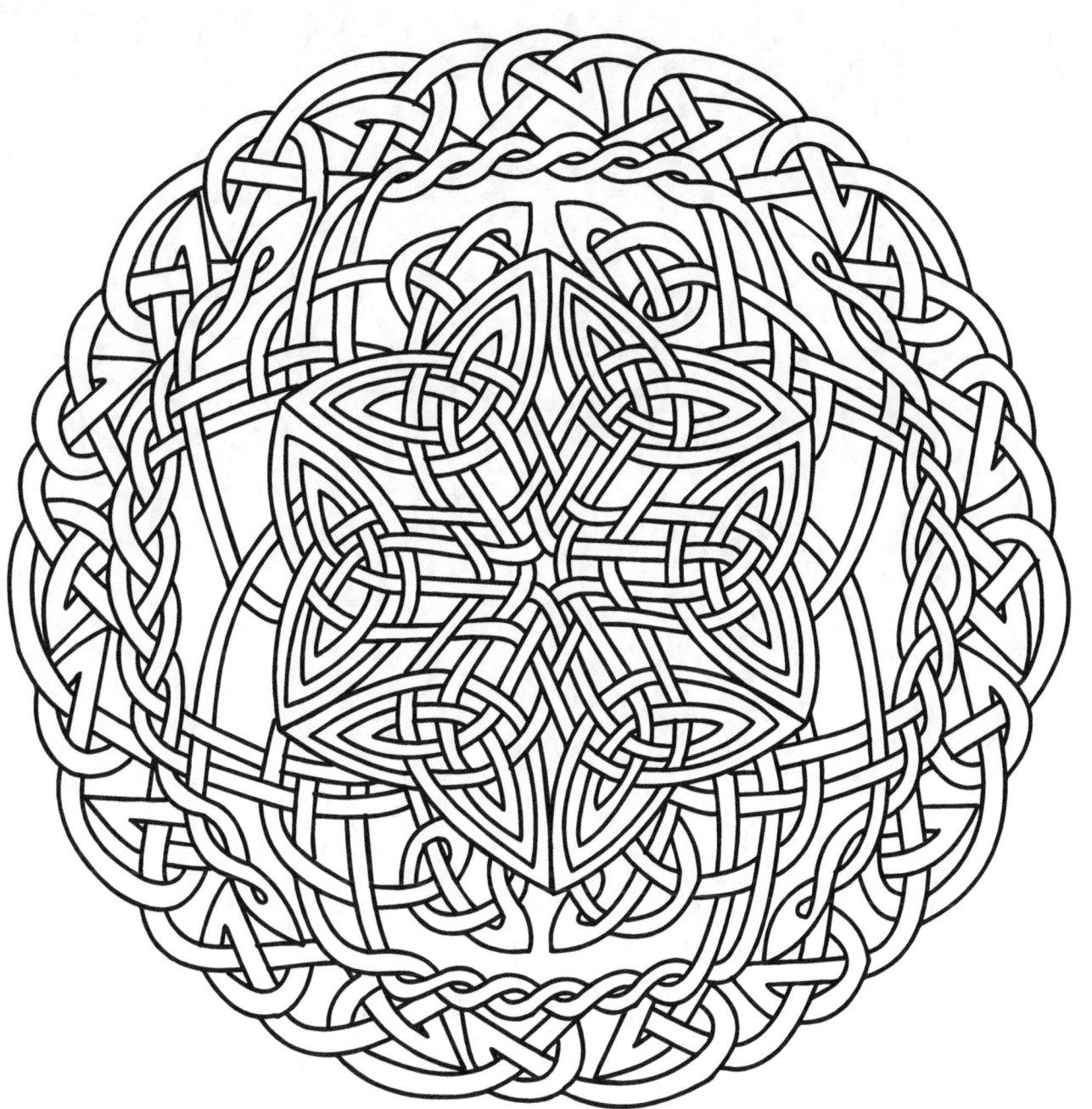

"I wonder if the World would feel differently about me if they could see how life feels viewing it like I do, through my eyes."

-Tina J. Richardson,

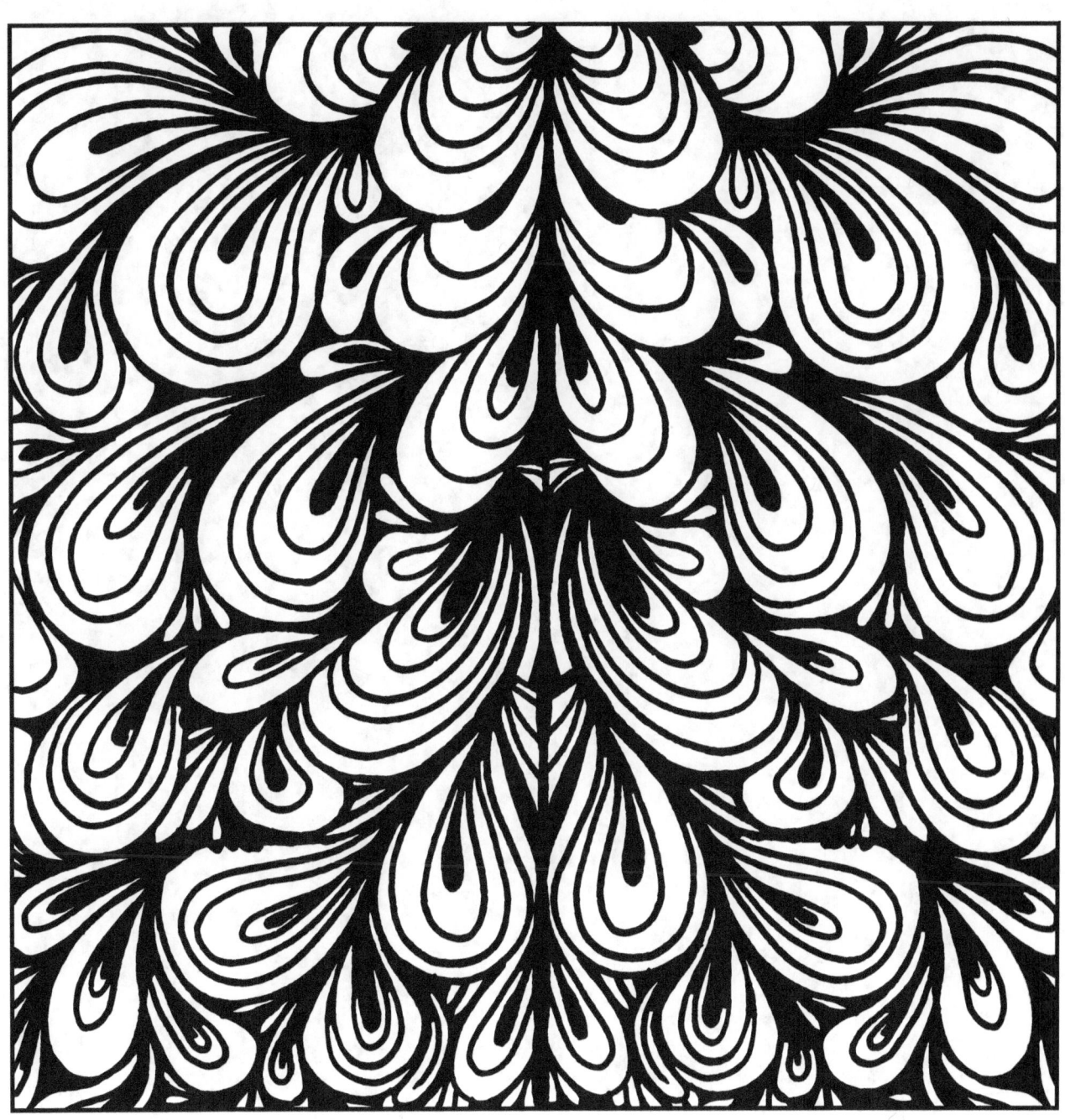

"Normal is a dryer setting."

- Elizabeth Moon

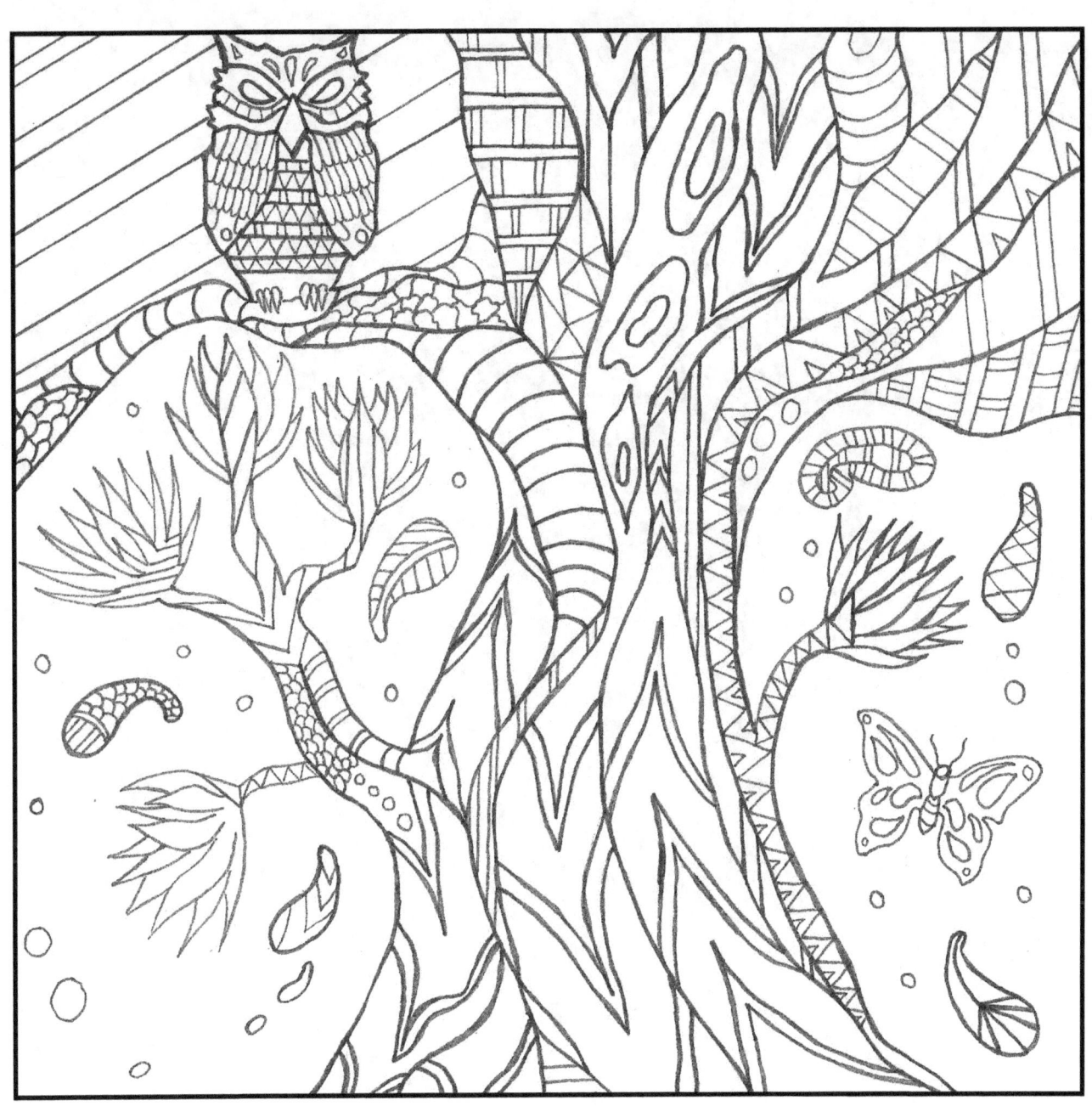

"Remember a person with Autism isn't a set of symptoms or statistics. Always remember and remind them that they're a person first."

- Paul Isaacs

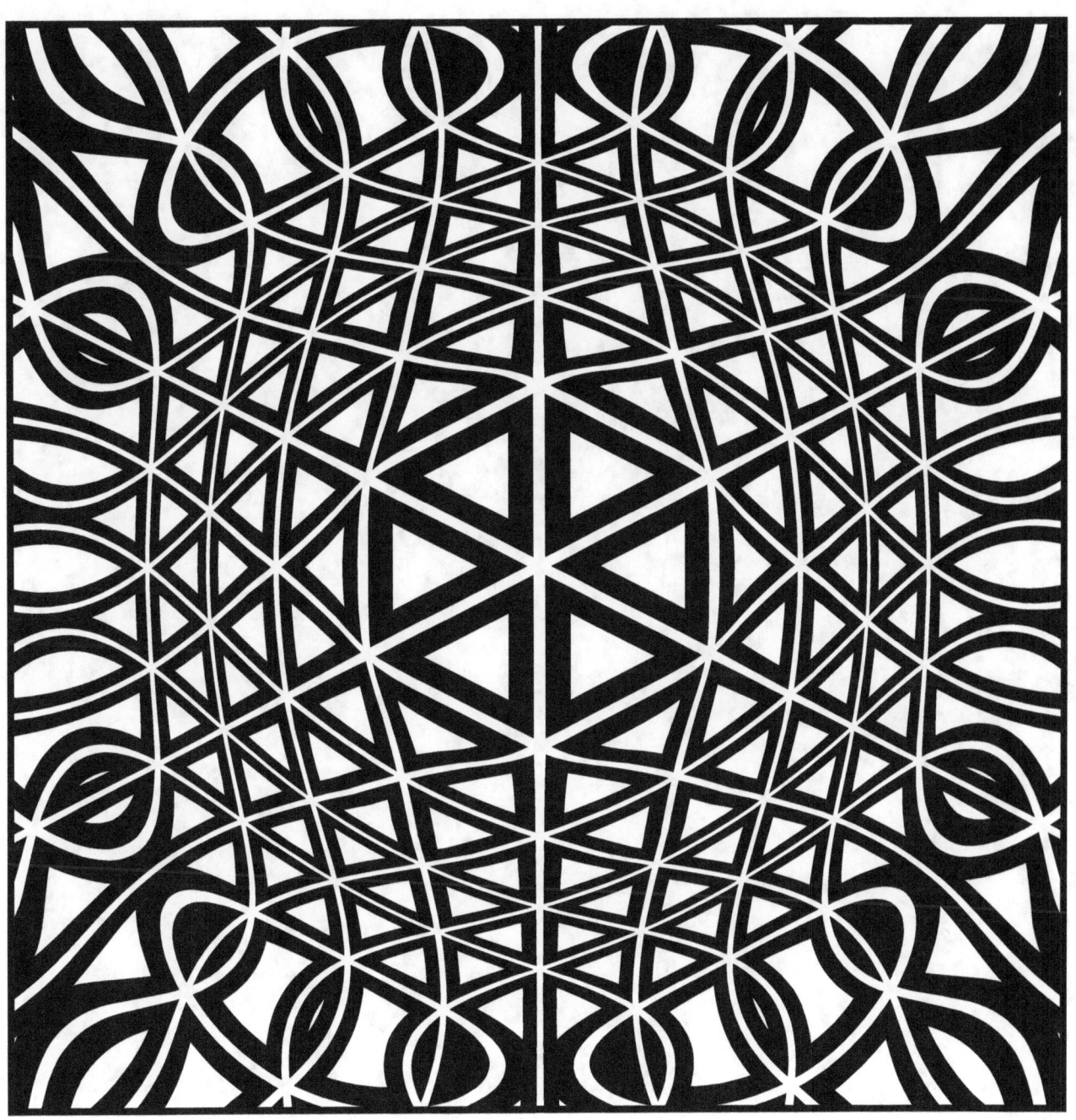

"Autism is not a processing error,
it is just a different operating system."

- Author Unknown

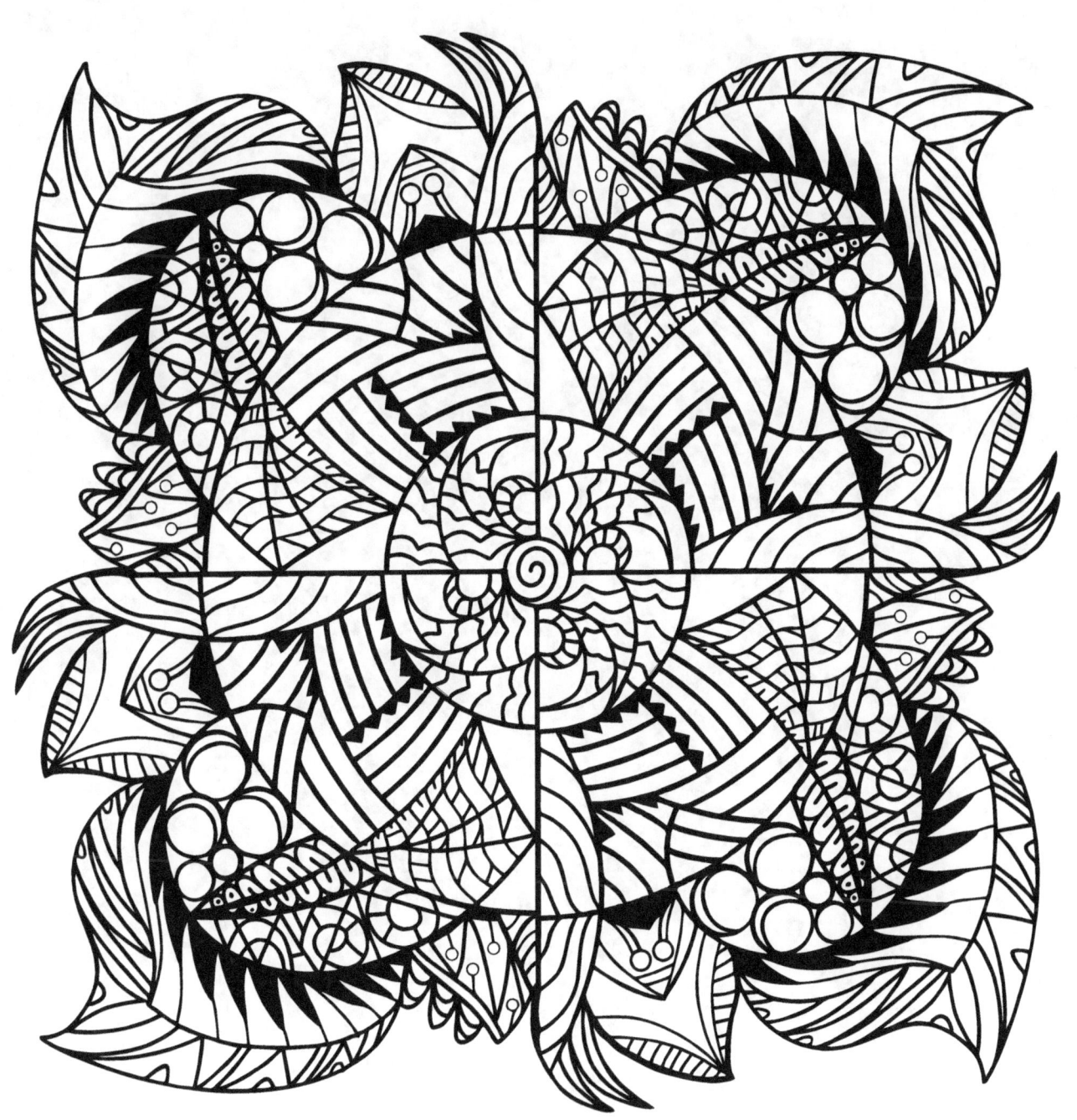

"Autistic people view the world in a different light, in ways many could never imagine."

- Tina J. Richardson

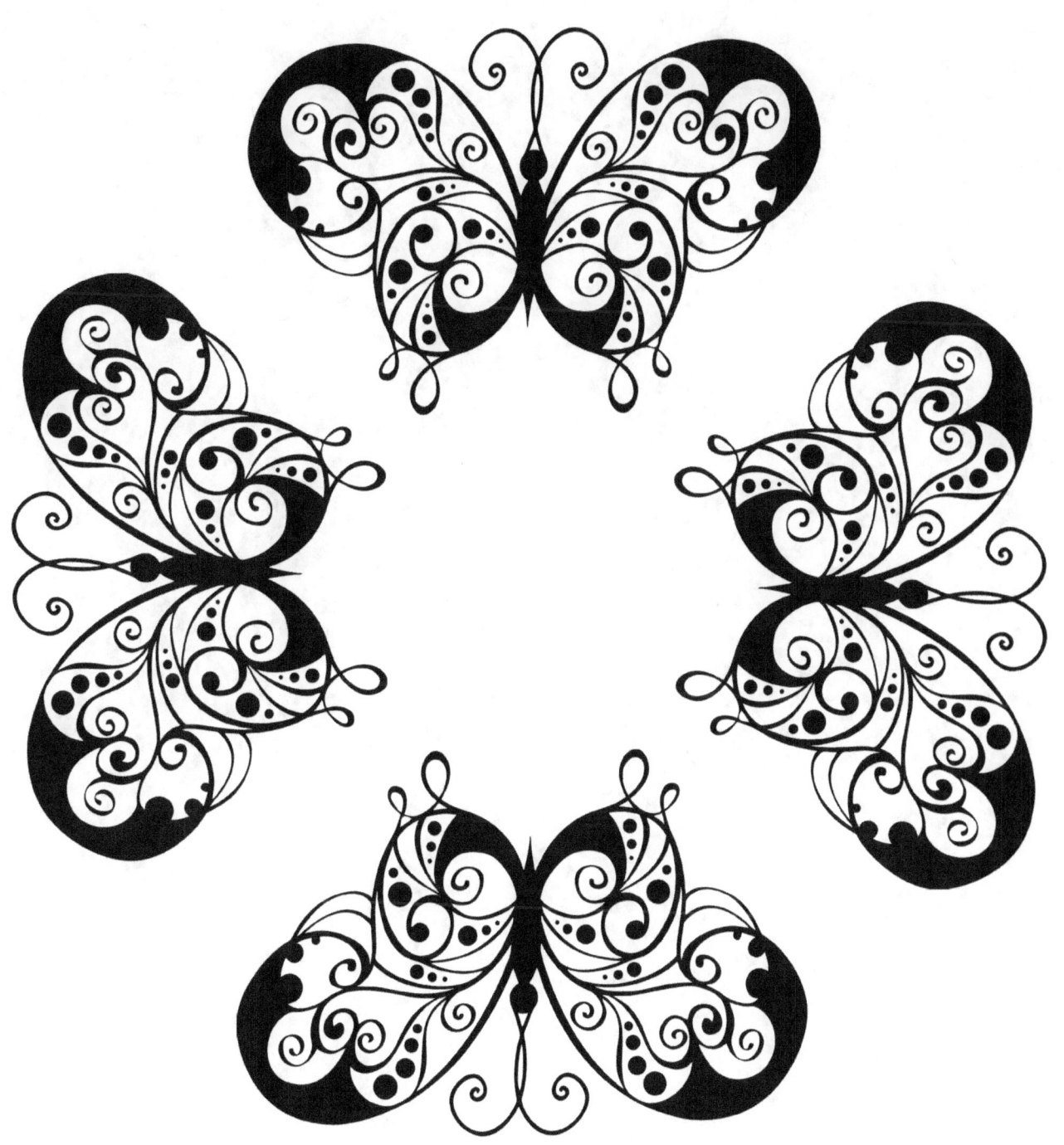

"Here's to a day that was free of any stress, meltdowns or major messes."

- said no parent of an Autistic child EVER

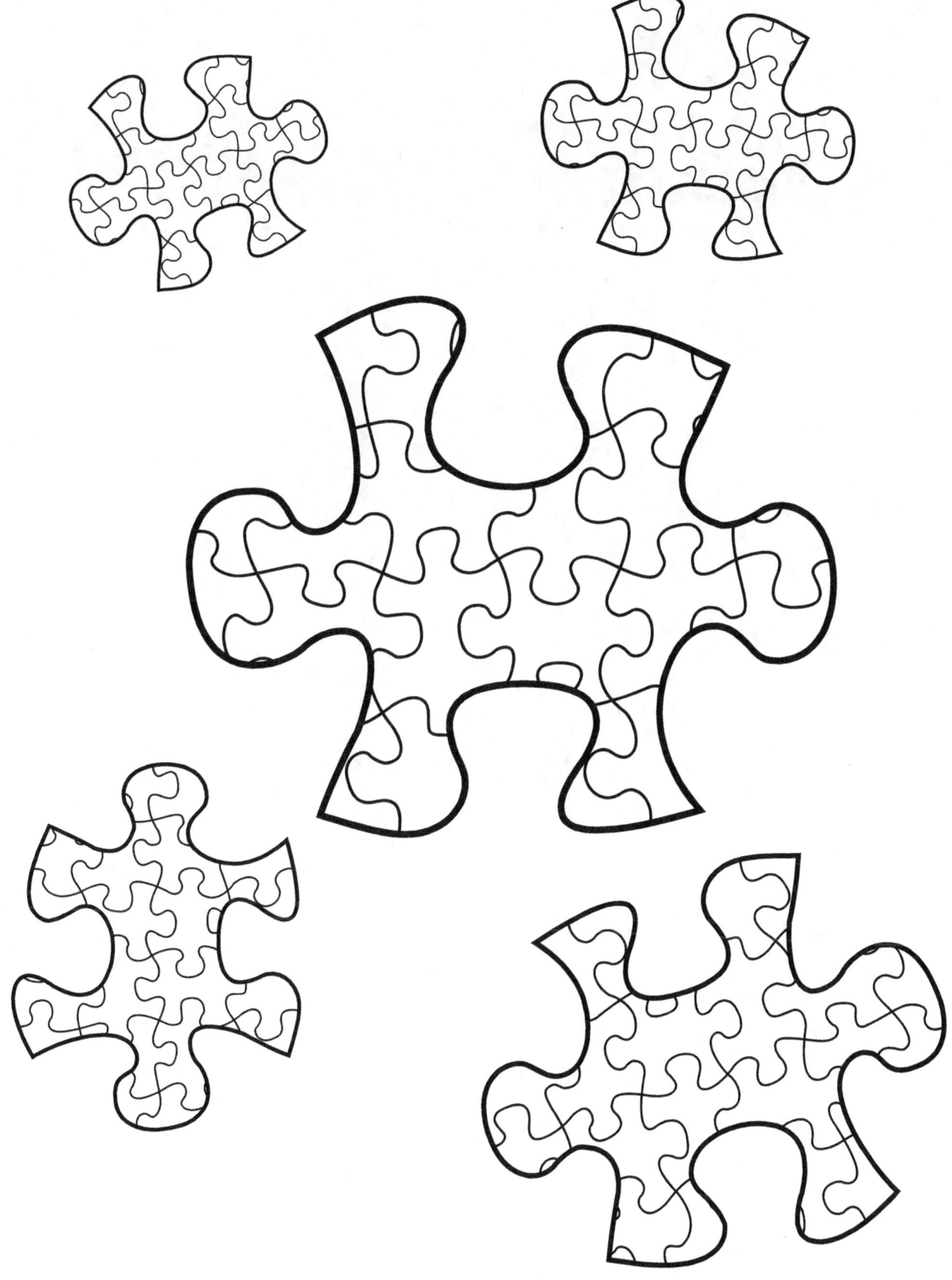

"Even for parents of children who are not on the spectrum, there is no such thing as a normal child."

- Violet Stevens

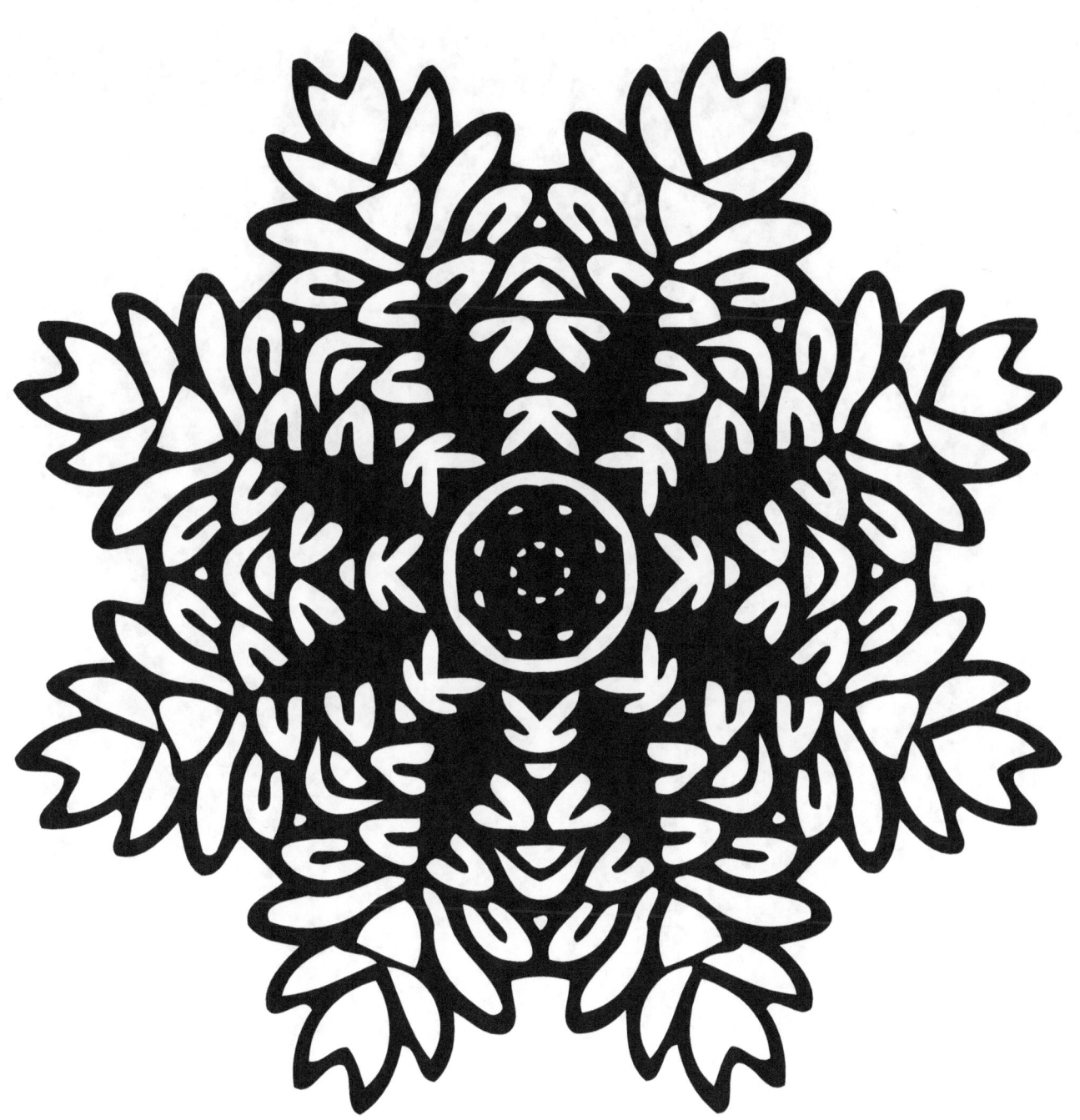

"If you've met one person with Autism,
you've met one person with Autism."

- Stephen Shore

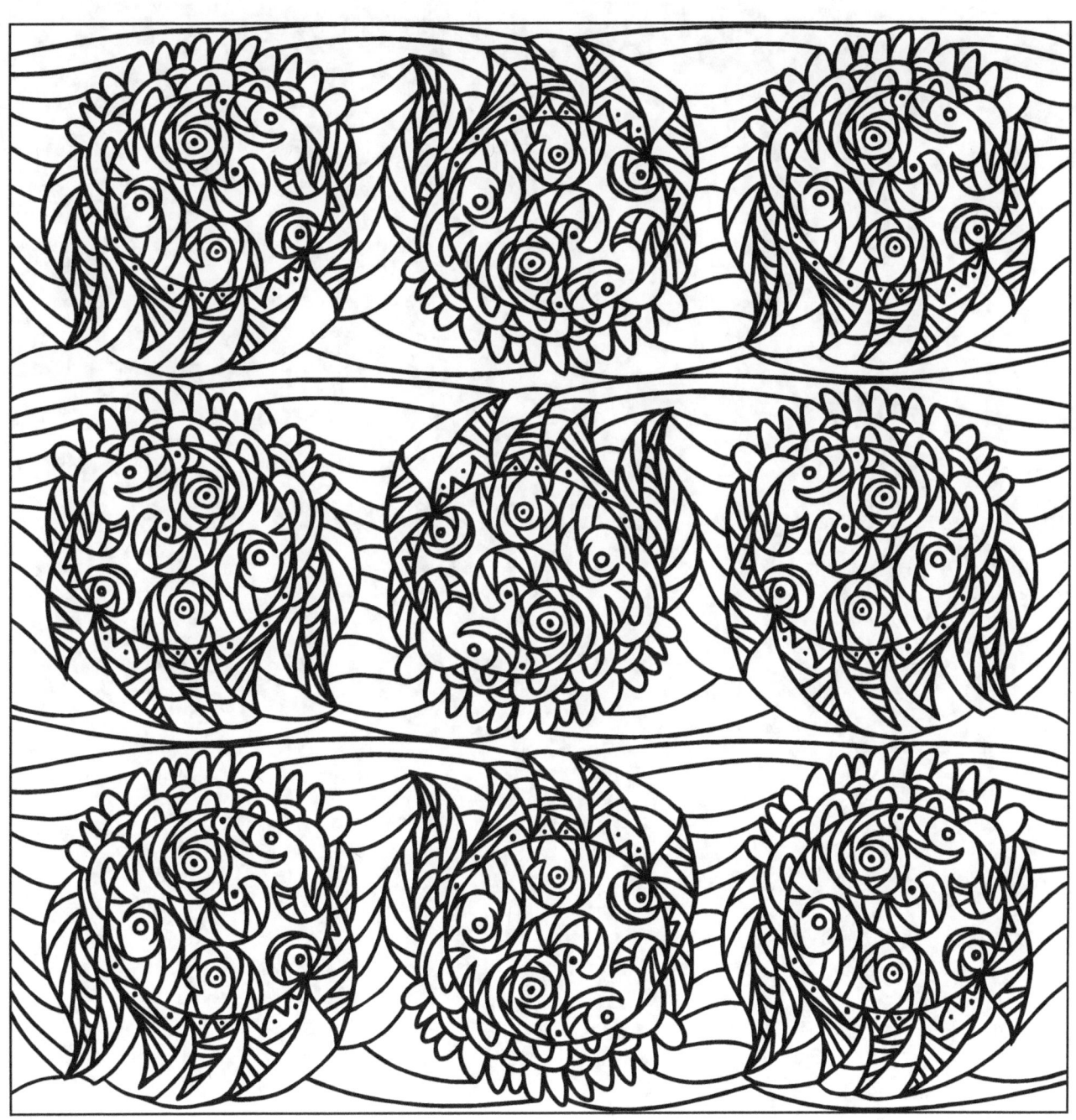

"Autism is more like retina patterns than measles."

- Naoki Higashida

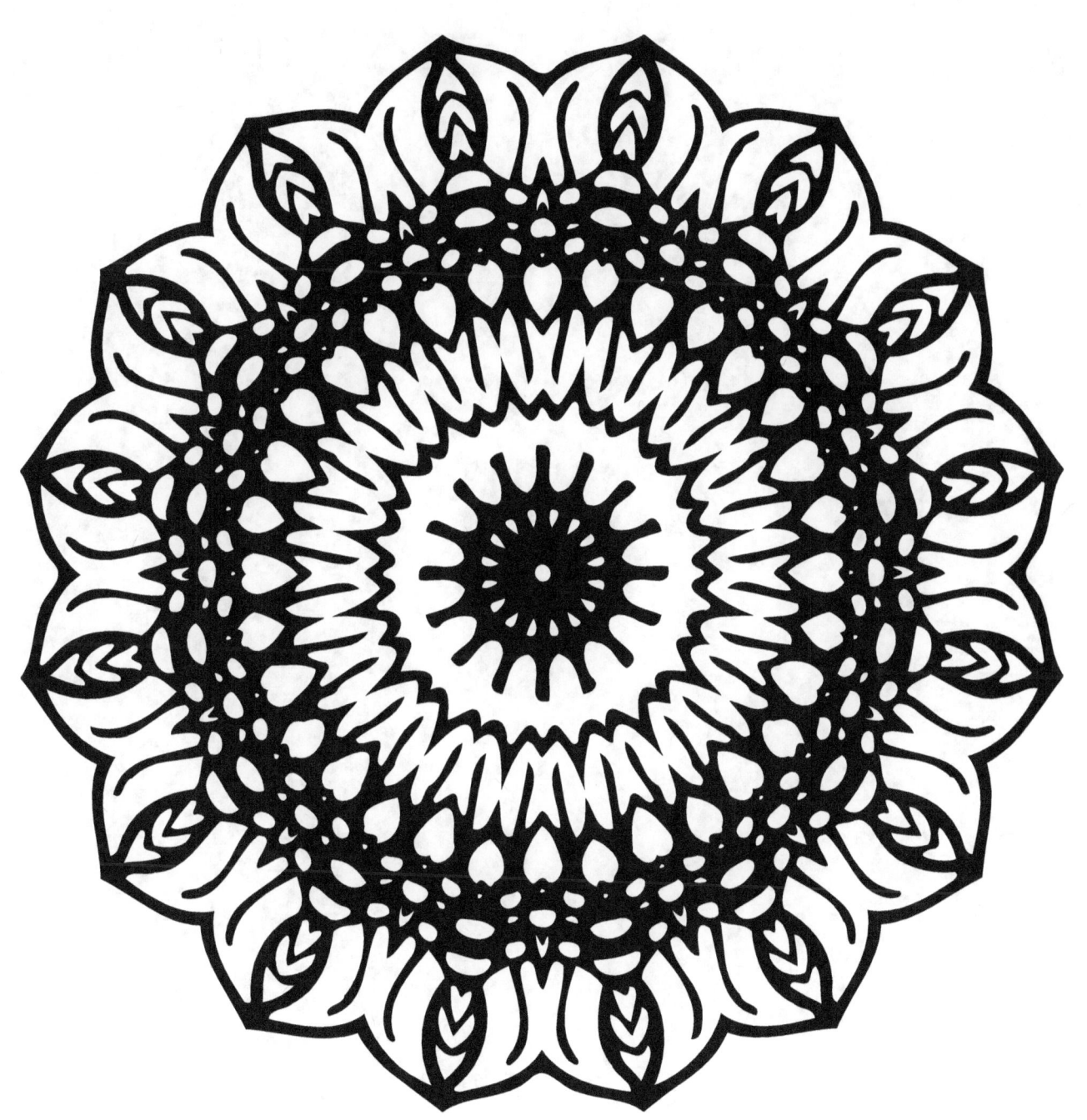

"Autism is one word attempting to describe millions of different stories."

- Stuart Duncan

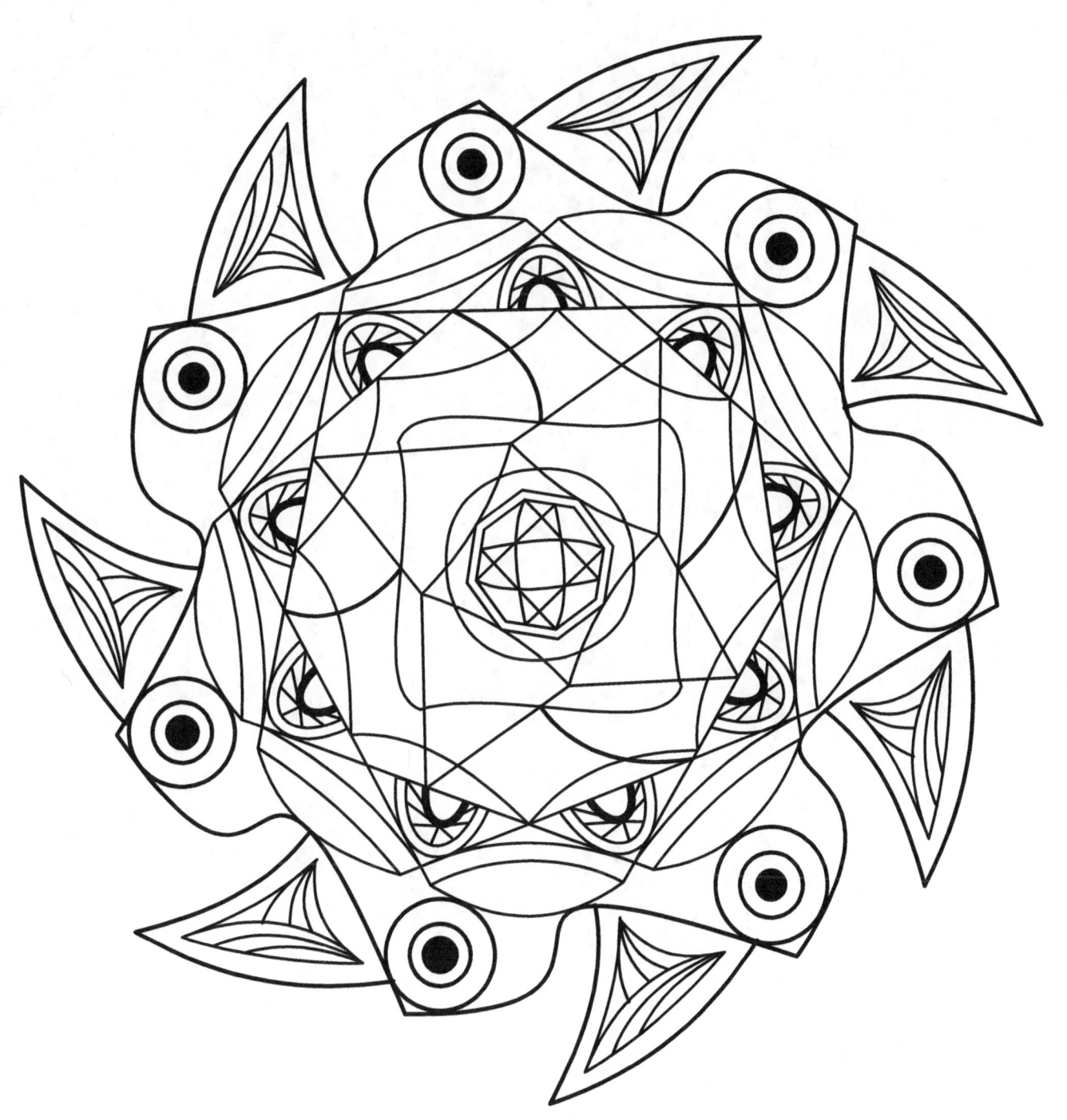

"If you can't see the gift in having a child with Autism, you're focusing too much on the Autism and not enough on the child."

- Stuart Duncan

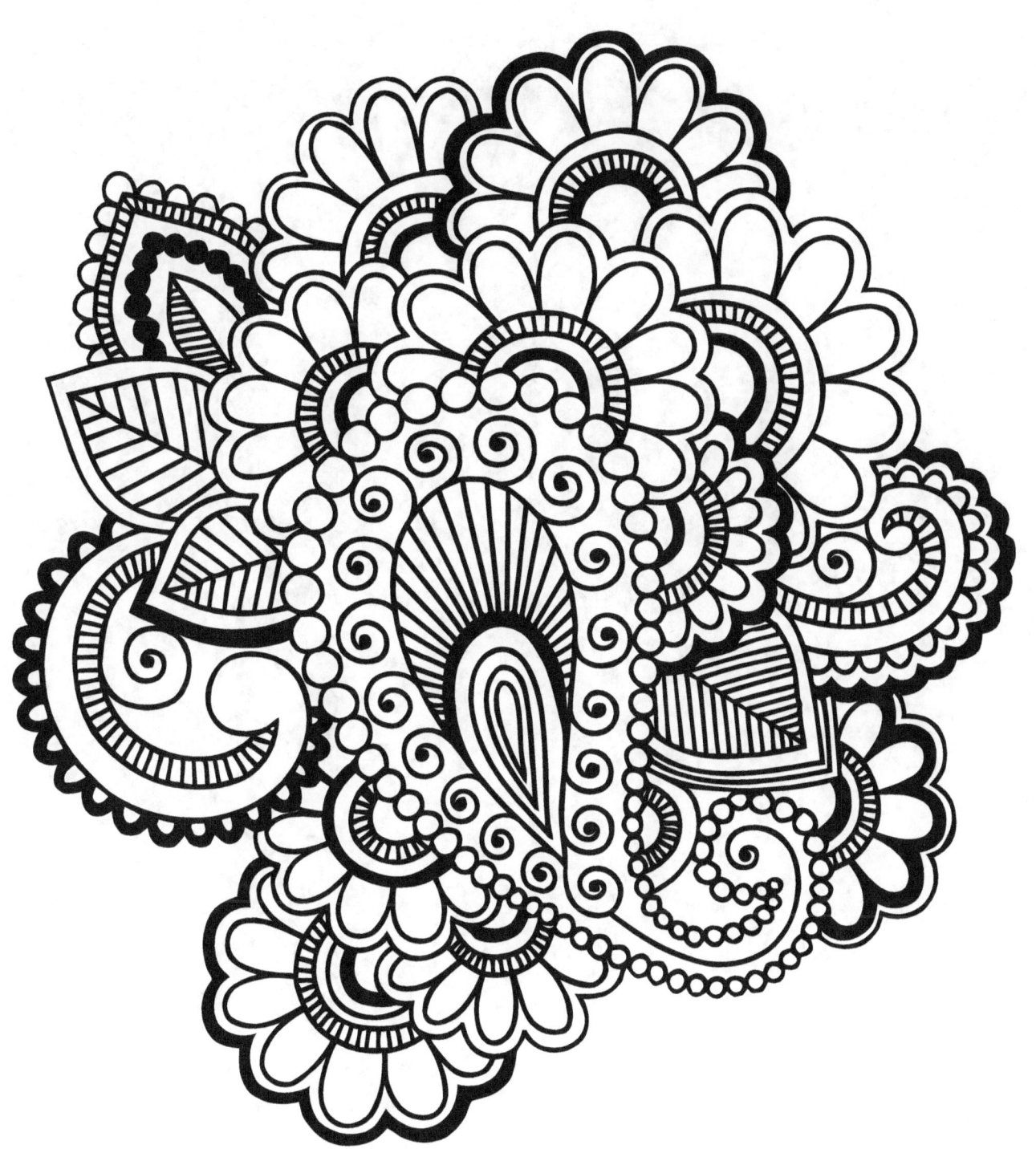

"Autism is part of my child, it's not everything he is. My child is so much more than a diagnosis."

-S.L. Coelho

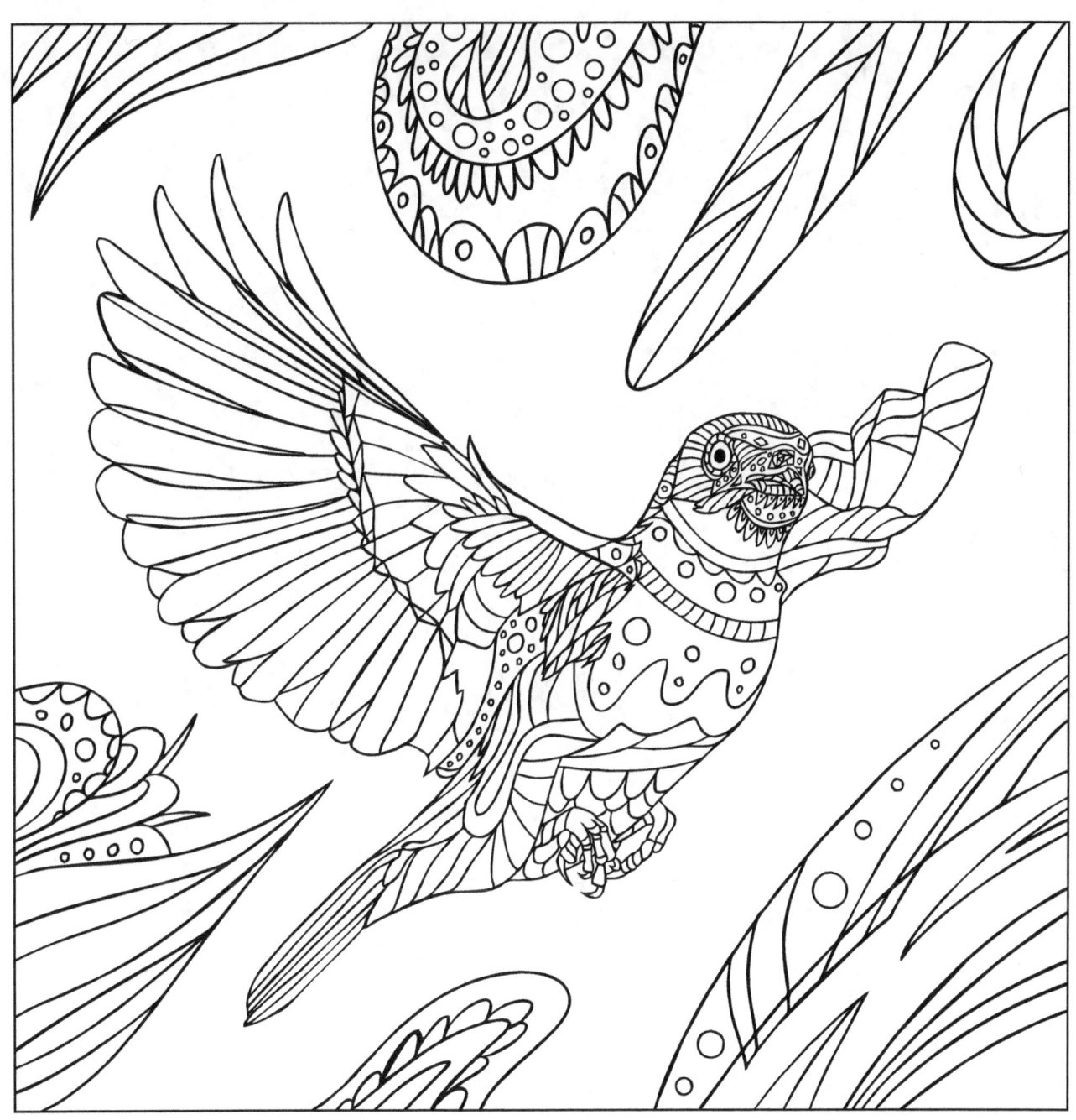

"It takes a village to raise a child. It takes a child with Autism to raise the consciousness of the village."

-Coach Elaine Hall

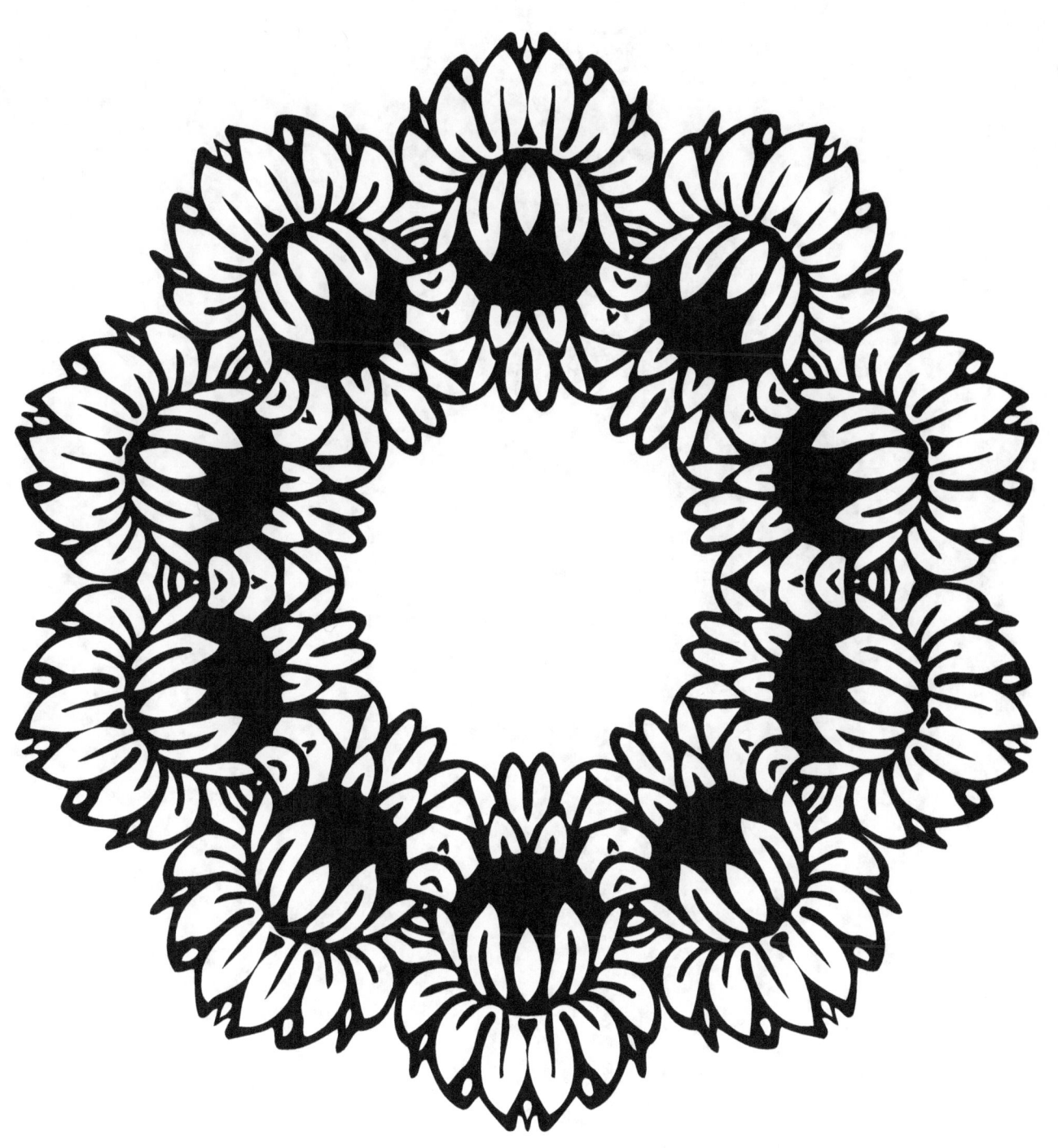

"Get to know someone on the spectrum and your life will truly be blessed!"

-Stephanie L. Parker

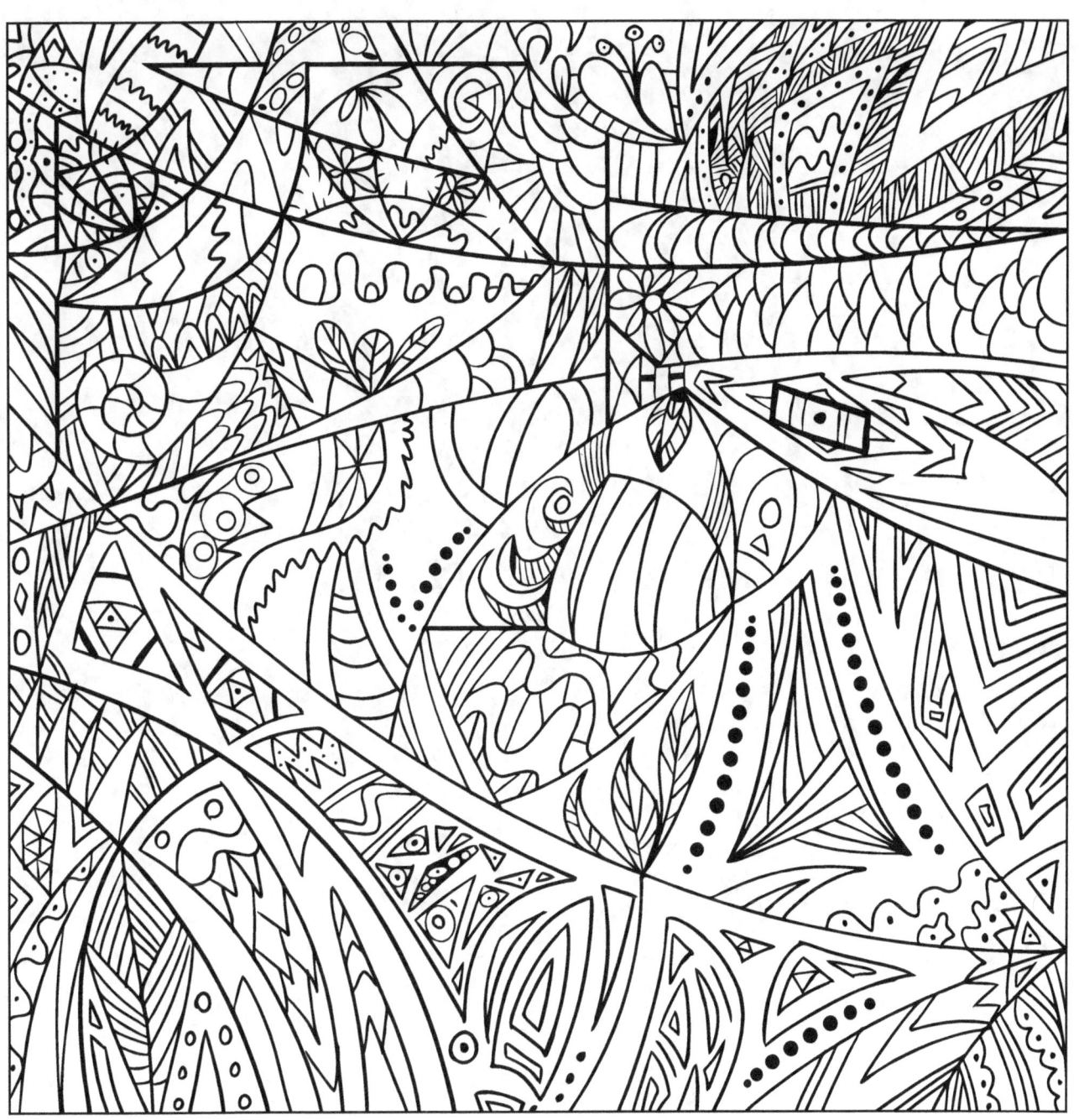

"Autism offers a chance for us to glimpse an awe-filled vision of the world that might otherwise pass us by."

- Dr. Colin Zimbleman, Ph.D.

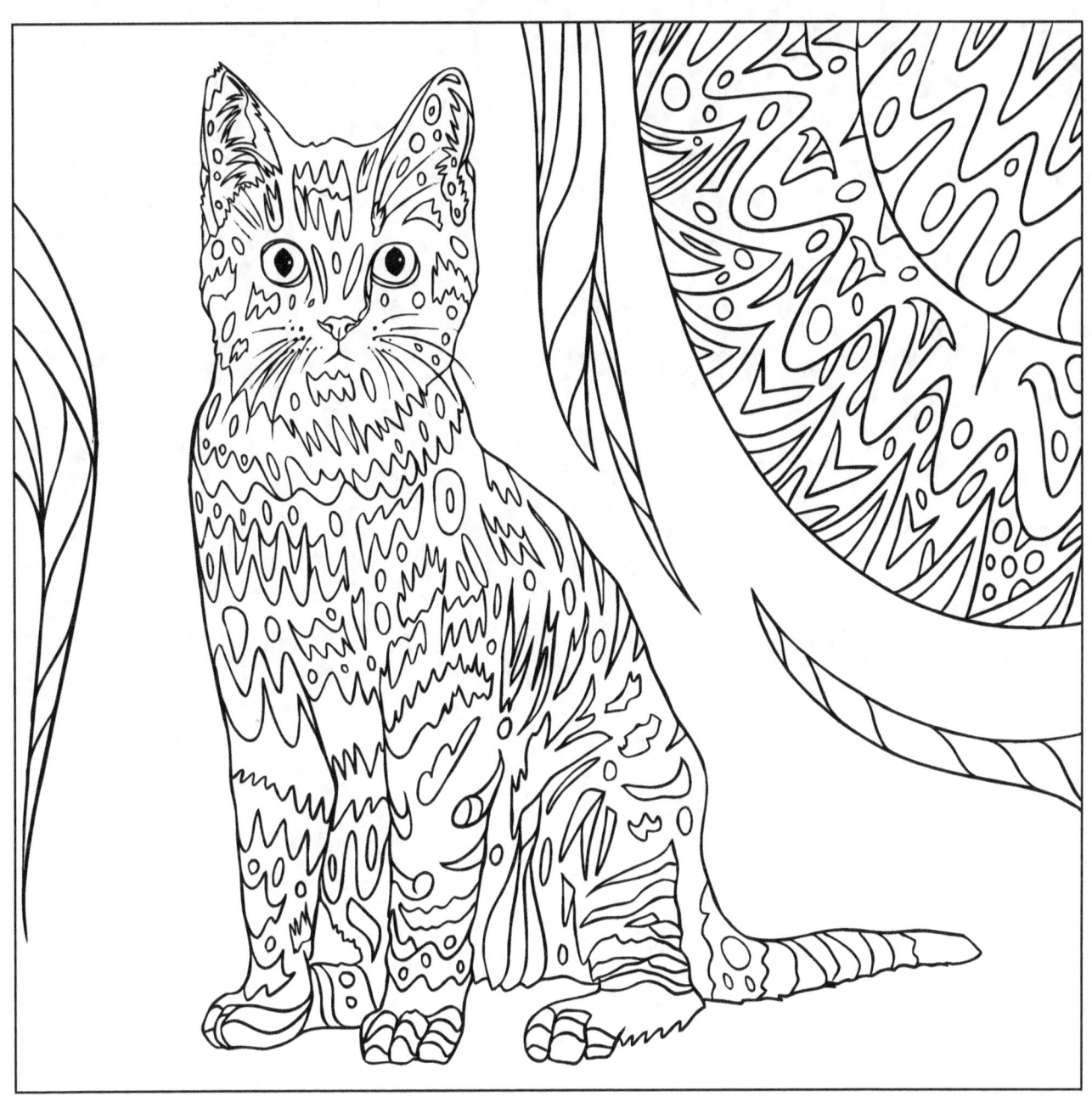

"The difference between high-functioning and low-functioning is that high-functioning means your deficits are ignored, and low-functioning means your assets are ignored."

– Laura Tisoncik

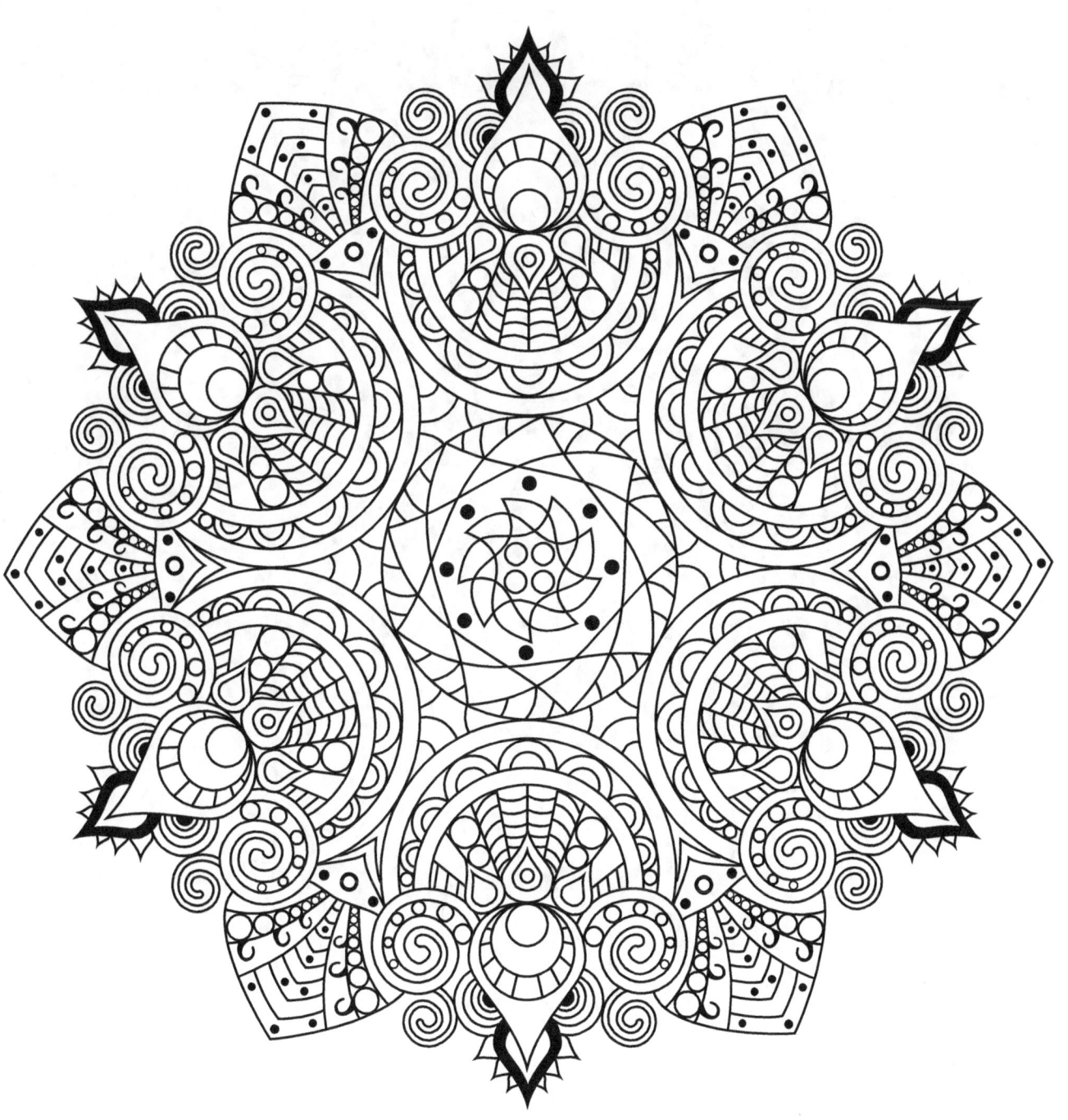

"What makes a child gifted and talented
may not always be good grades in school, but a different
way of looking at the world and learning."

-Chuck Grassley

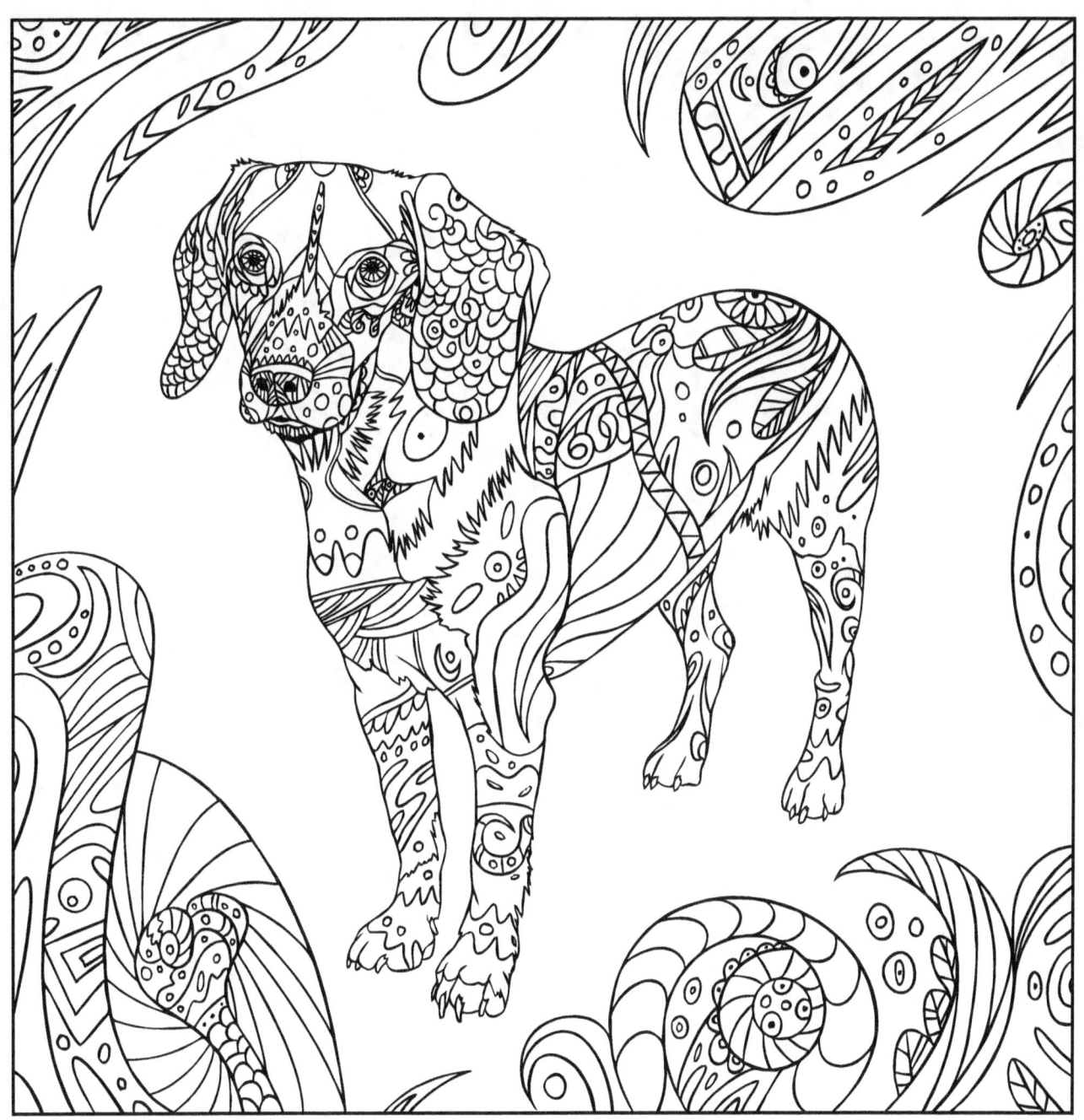

"Building up a weakness just makes you less disabled. Building a strength can take you to the top of the world."

- John Elder Robison

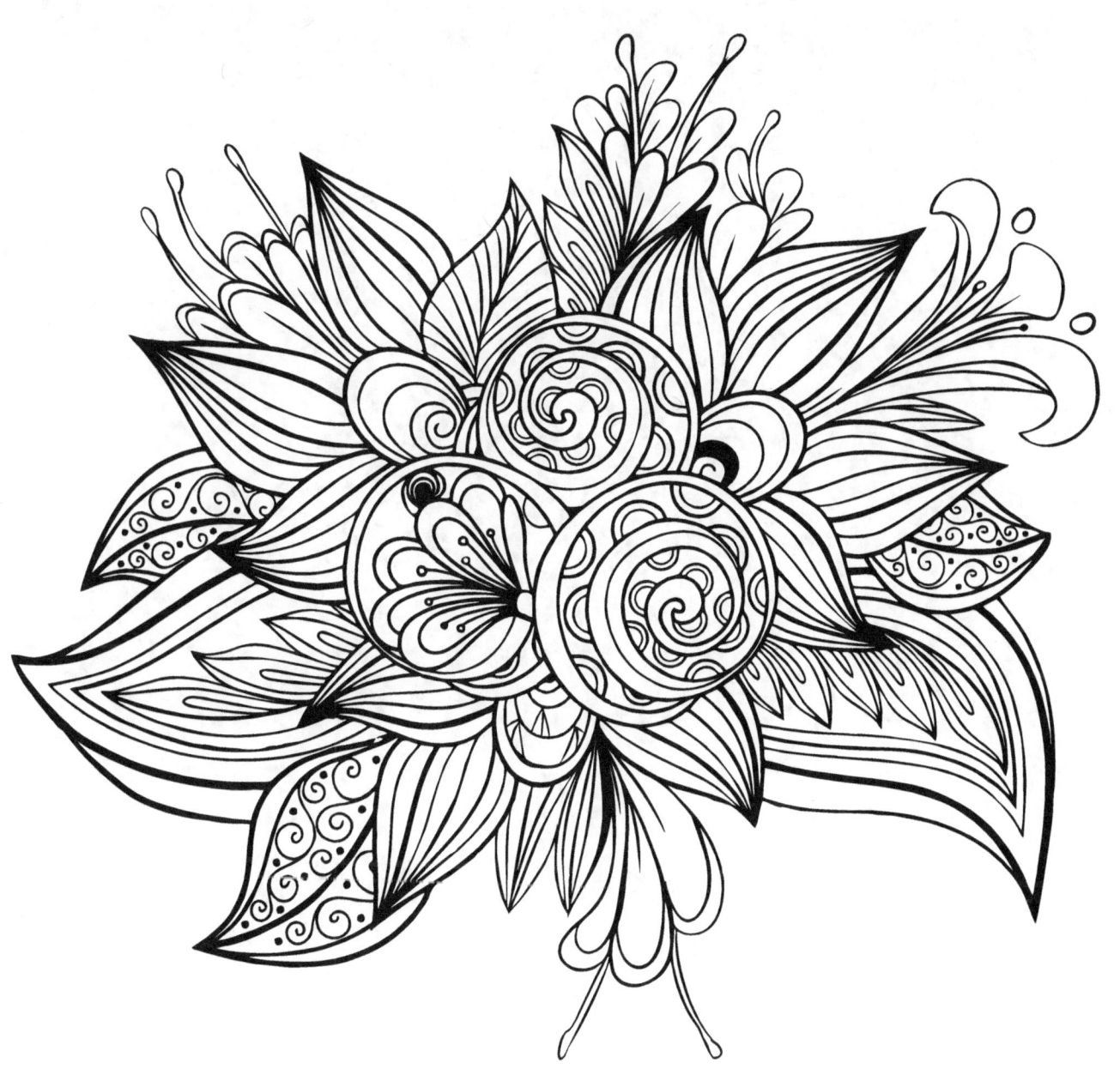

"I don't need Autism awareness,
Autism acceptance will do just fine."

- Jiheishou Daigakusha

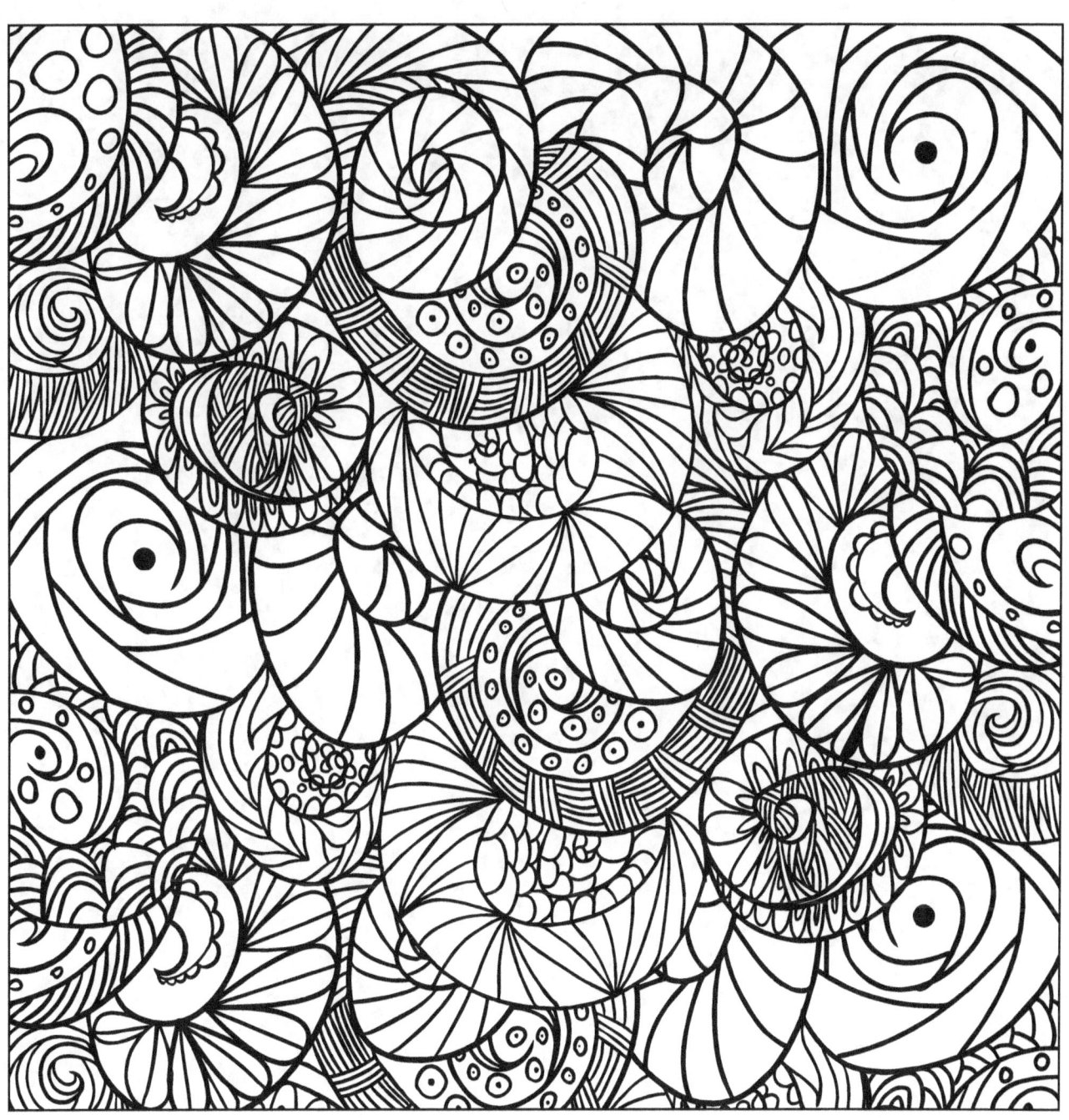

"It seems that for success in science or art,
a dash of Autism is essential."

- Hans Asperger.

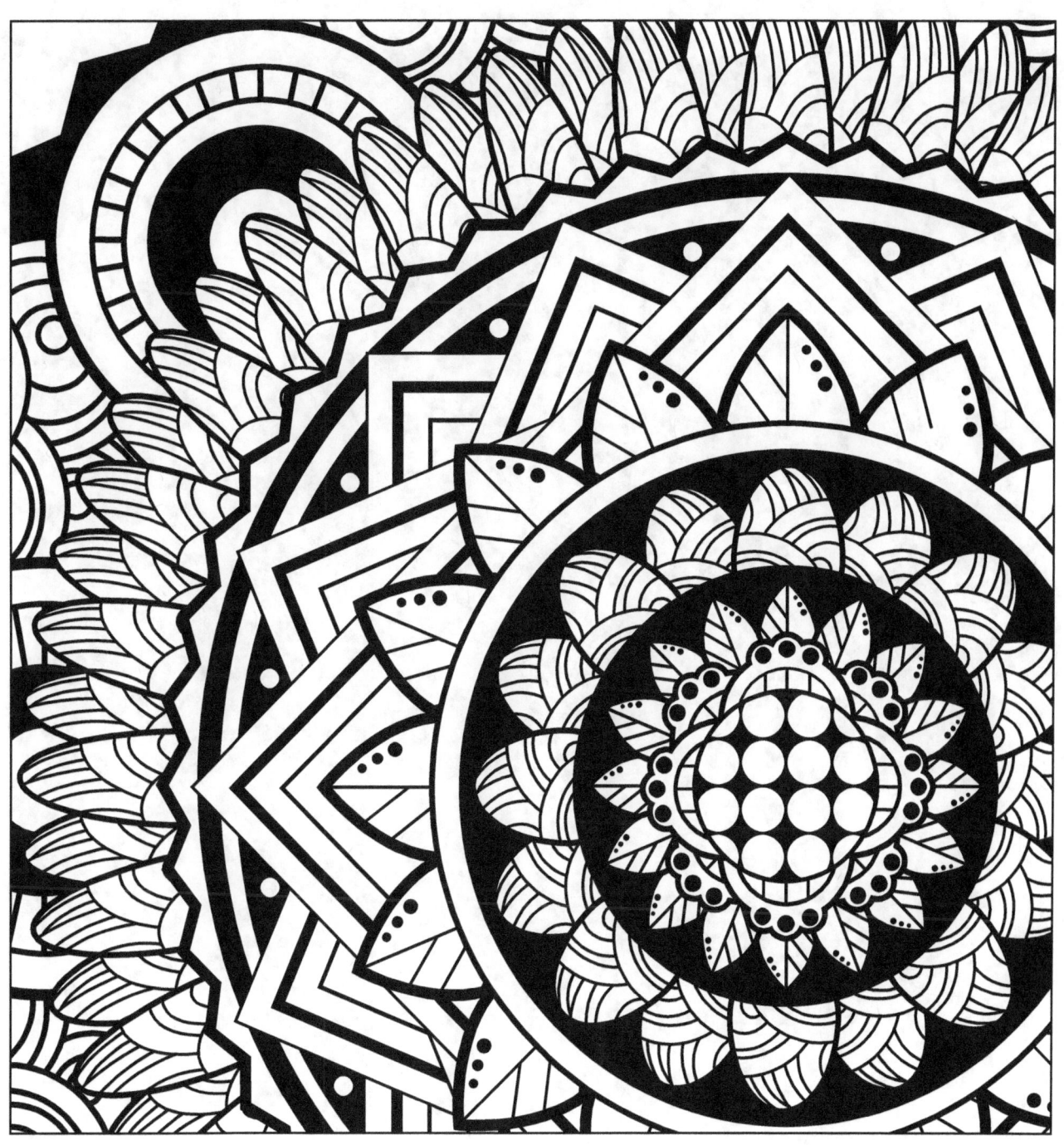

"Sometimes it is the people no one can imagine anything of who do the things no one can imagine."

– Alan Turing

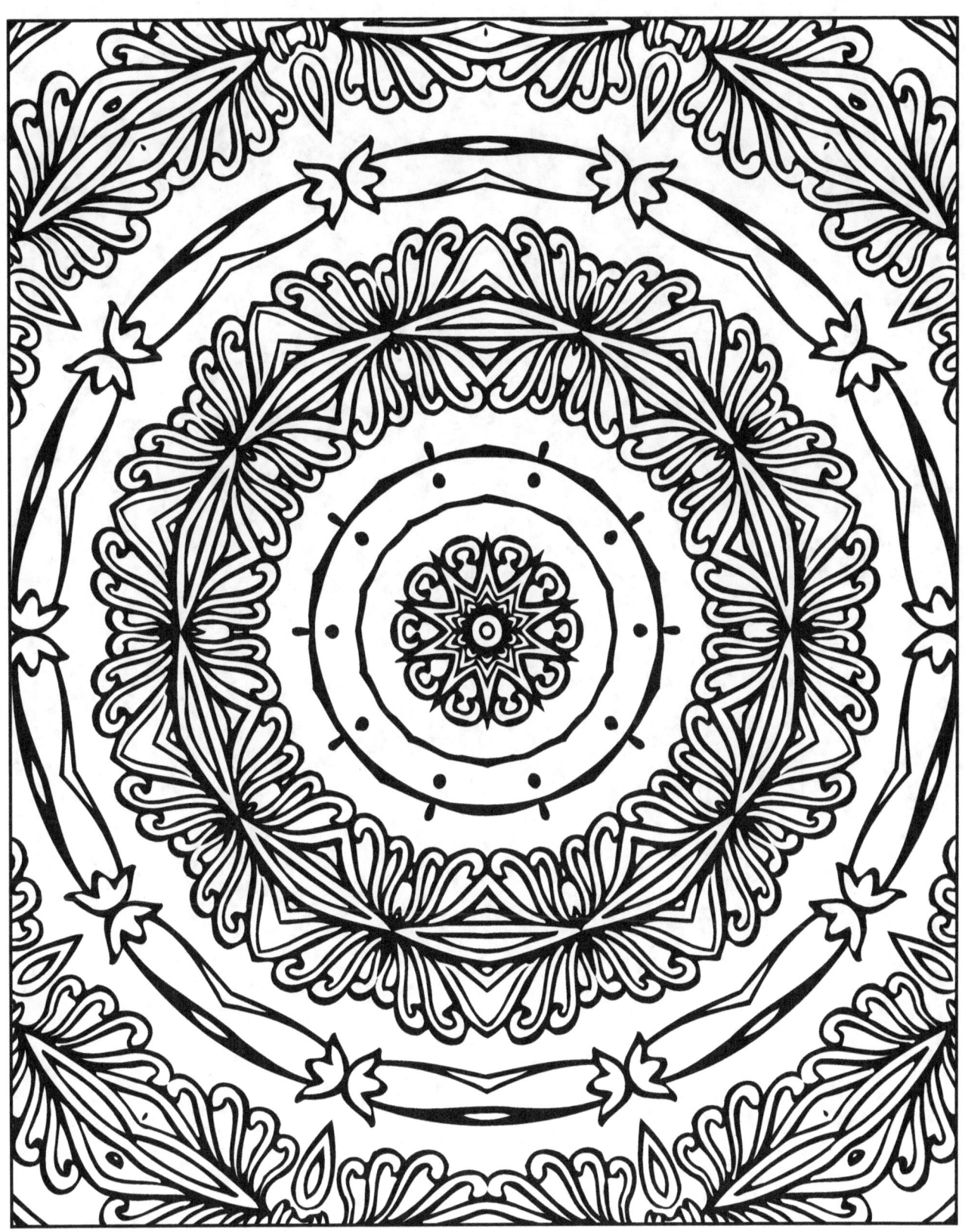

"Asperger's Syndrome - It worked for Einstein."

- Author Unknown

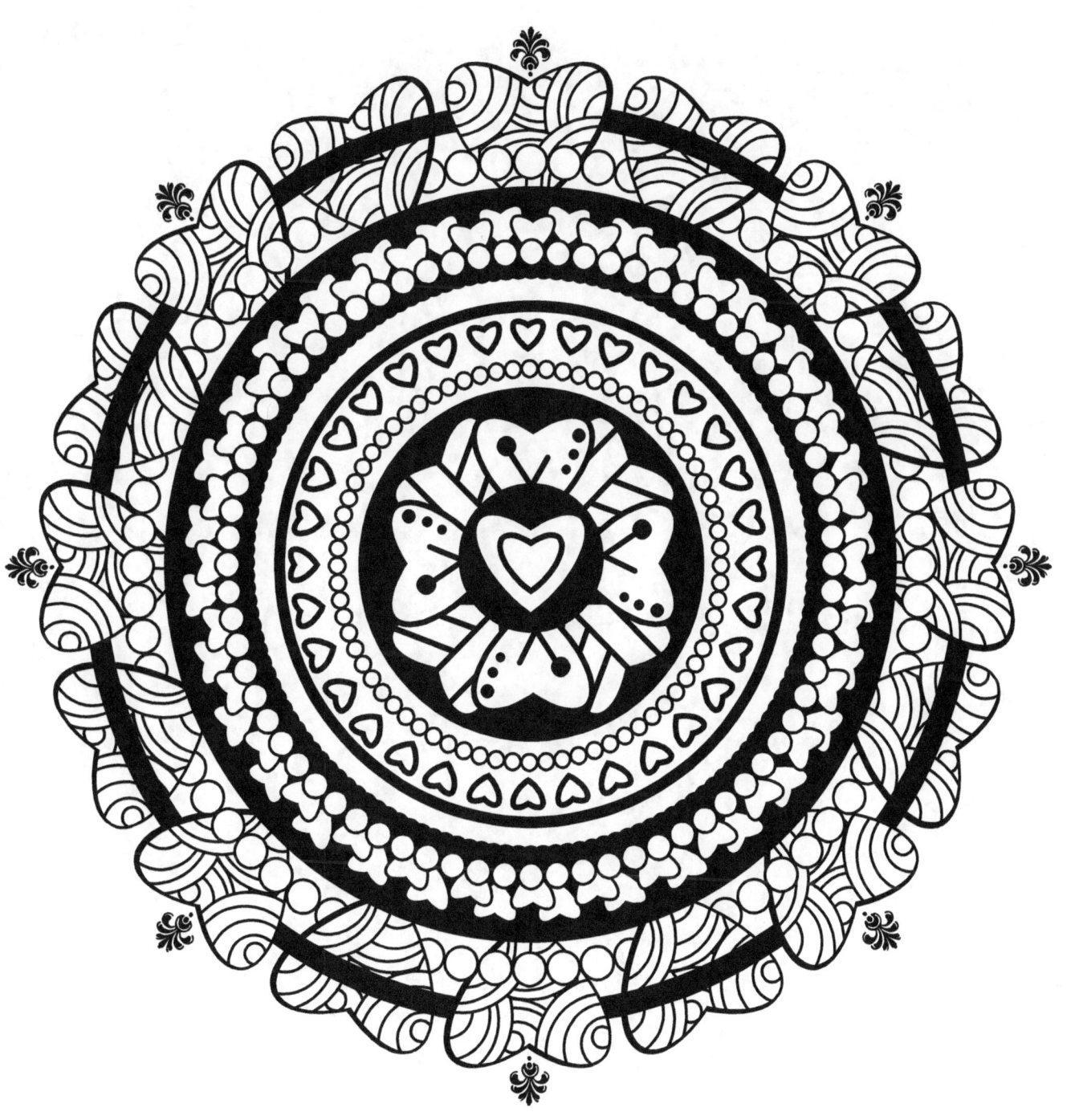

"I know of nobody who is purely Autistic
or purely neurotypical. Even God had some Autistic
moments, which is why the planets all spin."

– Jerry Newport

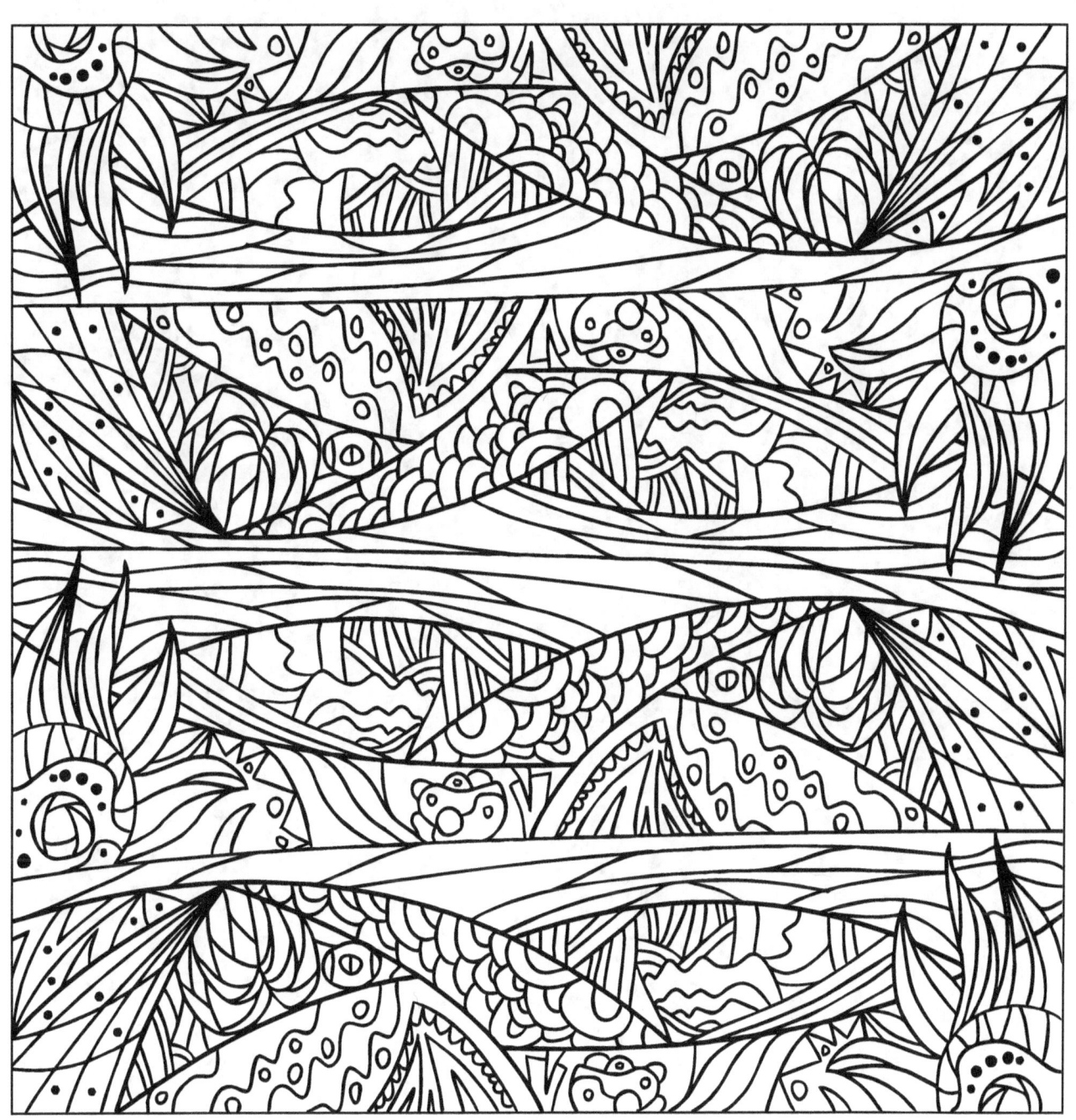

"What is important is to treat everyone like an individual and learning not to generalize Autism. With Autism, people make assumptions, but it's very broad, and everyone's so different. You have to treat each person as an individual."

- Nikki Reed

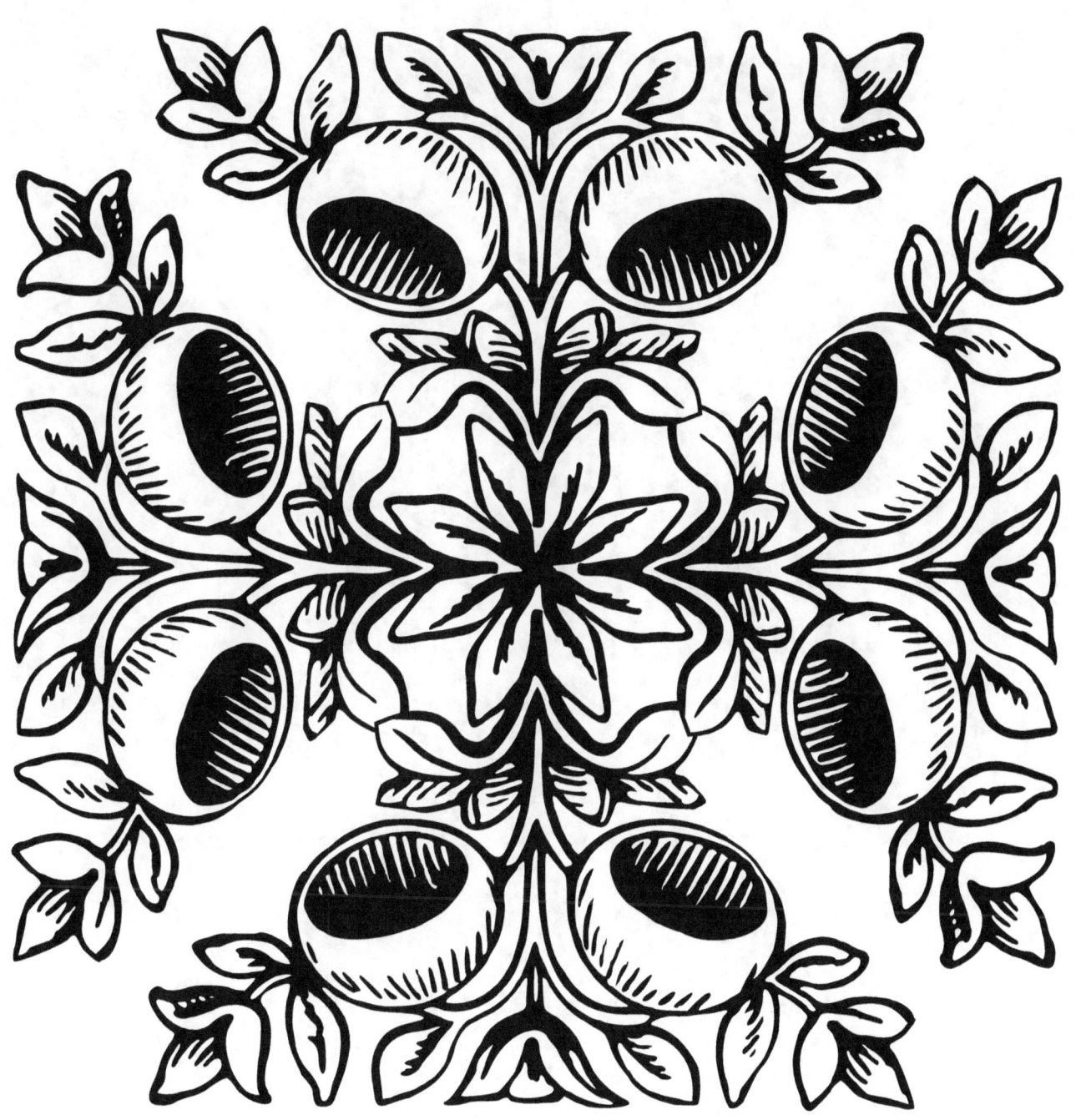

"Just because I can't speak doesn't mean
I have nothing to say!"

- Author Unknown

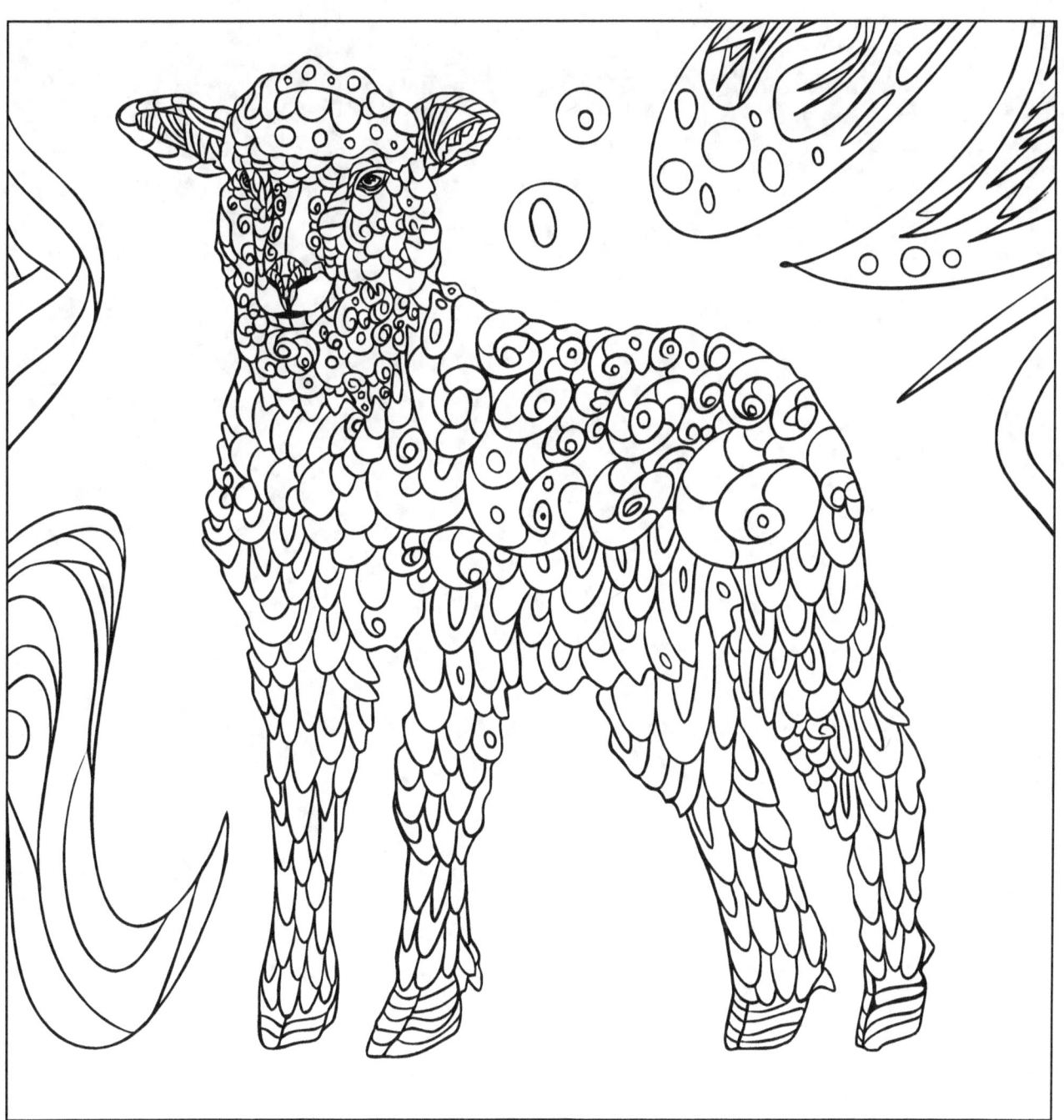

www.ingramcontent.com/pod-product-compliance
Lightning Source LLC
Chambersburg PA
CBHW080134240526
45468CB00009BA/2438